# EMERGENCY RESPONDER

## COMMUNICATION SKILLS HANDBOOK

How Your Words and Actions
Affect People in Medical Distress

Brian E Walsh PhD JP(Ret)

**WALSH**
seminars

PUBLISHING
HOUSE

**Copyright © 2010 Walsh Seminars Ltd.**

Cover designer: Derek Chiodo,
Cover illustrations: iStockphoto
Cover photo: fotolia
Internal illustrations and photographs: iStockphoto

**Library and Archives Canada Cataloguing in Publication**

Walsh, Brian Everard, 1947-
    Emergency responders communication skills handbook : how your words and actions affect people in distress / Brian E. Walsh.

Includes index.
ISBN 978-0-9866655-0-9

    1. First responders--Psychology--Handbooks, manuals, etc.
2. Emergency management--Psychological aspects--Handbooks, manuals, etc. 3. Interpersonal communication--Handbooks, manuals, etc. I. Title.

BF789.D5W33 2010       363.34'019       C2010-904689-7

Walsh Seminars Ltd.
Box 963  Victoria BC V8W 2R9 Canada
www.WalshSeminars.com

Book website:  www.ERcommSkills.com

Printed in the United States of America and the United Kingdom.

# Acknowledgements

I would like to express my sincere appreciation to the many who contributed as editors, proofreaders, and technical advisors.

Senior Editors:
Astrid Whiting, Medical Exercise Specialist
Andrew Cowie, Primary Care Paramedic (IV)
R.G. Willard, a trusted Australian colleague from my China days
Ted Roberts BComm MBA, author (Canada)

- Alaa M. Morsi PhD, Psychologist, NLP and Hypnotherapy Trainer (Egypt)
- Andrew P. Horton PhD, Neurolinguistic Programming Trainer (USA)
- Blair Harvey BA, Sergeant, Emergency Planning, Research & Planning Unit, London Police Service (Canada)
- Brent Shea BA MPA, Superintendent, London Police Service (Canada)
- Brett Fryer, Inspector, Saanich Police (Canada)
- Dr. Brian S. Pound, Family Physician & Hypnotherapist, Associate Professor, School of Nursing, University of Victoria (Canada)
- Darel Ellert, Life Coach and Energy Psychology Practitioner (Canada)
- David M. Quintana, Denver Fire Department, Div. Chief of Safety & Training
- Deana Ryan PhD, Faculty, Kona University, (USA)
- Donna Saltman, Emergency Management and Business Continuity, Vancouver Island Health Authority (Canada)
- Gregg Turner BA, therapist and executive coach (Canada)
- Jeffrey S. Katz, M.S., Lieutenant, Boynton Beach Police Department; doctoral student, Walden University (USA)
- Jim Christie, Operations Manager, Middlesex London EMS (Canada)
- Jim Stanton, crisis communications specialist  (Canada)
- John Ryan PhD, Faculty, Kona University, (USA)
- Kenneth J. Maloney, National Ski Patrol (USA)
- Michael R. Eslinger, RN, CRNA, MA, APN, BCH, CMI, Captain, USN Retired President and CEO American Association of Moderate Sedation Nurses, Inc.
- Dr. Nathalie Fiset, Family Physician & Hypnotherapist (Canada)
- Peter Hicks BA, retired corrections officer, probation-parole worker (Canada)
- Portia Dewhirst, MA, Director of Programs, Canadian Police Sector Council
- Will Stovall BA, retired Military Police officer, school district Crisis Management Coordinator (USA)

*Dedicated to the courageous
emergency responders
who serve us on the
front lines of our streets.*

*And also saluting all those
volunteers who give their
valuable time as*

*First aiders
Disaster relief workers
Search and Rescue members*

*and in other capacities, at their
own expense, and often without
recognition or appreciation.*

iv

Born in the U.K. and raised in Canada near Montreal, Brian Walsh was a journalist and broadcaster before joining a major international firm. For much of his thirty-year career he was involved in human resources, specifically staff training.

While living in the Canadian Arctic, Brian served as a Justice of the Peace, and studied anthropology and Neurolinguistic Programming (NLP). Those experiences and extensive international travel prepared him for working with other cultures. He was then transferred to China where he served as his company's General Manager.

After his return to North America, he elected early retirement to further his earlier interest in NLP and hypnotherapy. He returned to formal study, and within four years had achieved his Ph.D. His dissertation, which focused on accelerated learning techniques, inspired his passion and his bestselling book, "Unleashing Your Brilliance." The companion video DVD for his book is "Enriched Learning."

Brian is dedicated to personal growth and enrichment through his workshops, teleclasses, audio and video products, and his many articles.

In addition, he has co-authored a self-help book with John Gray and Jack Canfield: "101 Great Ways to Improve Your Life."

He is an NLP Master Practitioner, a Clinical Hypnotherapist, an EFT Practitioner, and an Acupuncture Detoxification Specialist.

# Foreword by Lt. Jeffrey Katz

*What we have done for ourselves alone dies with us;*
*what we have done for others and the world remains and is immortal.*
Albert Pike

Think back to the beginning of your career. Do you remember the excitement you experienced when it came time to intervene in an emergency? Despite this initial excitement, if you are like most rescue personnel, these experiences have become increasingly less thrilling over time. Psychologists refer to this as "habituation" and it is completely normal. Habituation occurs when exposure to certain stimuli – in this case, life and death situations – causes us to view these incidents as commonplace.

It is important to remember that while you play a role in many of the emergencies in your community, the people you help are not typically habituated to crisis. This is a critical distinction because it underscores the paradox between your concept of *routine* and what others may consider a *life-changing event.*

You may be asking yourself why this little nugget of psychological insight is important to emergency services personnel. After all, chances are you are paid to lock up criminals, extinguish fires, or aid the injured. Technically, these courageous acts do not require conscious insight into the workings of the mind. Similarly, you do not need to have a stethoscope to check a patient's pulse, an automobile to chase down a fleeing burglar, or a ladder truck to extinguish a two-story apartment fire... but wouldn't these supplemental tools maximize the likelihood of your success?

The insights shared by Dr. Walsh are intended to augment your existing skills and enhance crucial *people-helping* competencies. Irrespective of our specialization, each of us is charged with interceding in crisis and restoring equilibrium to our respective communities. This process begins and ends with effective interpersonal interaction. The information contained within this Handbook will prove useful in several ways:

**Enhance the likelihood of contributing to someone's recovery.**
In our basic training, many of us learned that persons with survivable injuries might actually die of shock. We often help people who are impacted by sudden and traumatic events. The unexpected nature of these events complicates the psychological impact suffered by survivors. Emergency personnel who calm and reassure victims will help them combat the perils of shock. This is one of the underlying themes espoused by Dr. Walsh and arguably a valuable professional tool.

**Avoid unwarranted complaints.**
Has a citizen ever mistaken your steely demeanor for indifference or apathy? Has well-intended humor ever come back to haunt you? Has your behavior ever been misinterpreted? Remember, we tend to judge ourselves by our intentions while others judge us by our actions. In order to effectively help others, we must learn to demonstrate behavior congruent with our intentions and consistent with the expectations of those in crisis. This is easier said than done! Such an alignment is only possible through keen self-awareness and a conscious understanding of many of the interpersonal dynamics covered within this book.

**Increase support for your organization.**
Perhaps now more than ever, as the public becomes increasingly – and rightfully – insistent on maximizing the value of their tax dollars, customer service is essential in our line of work. For example, research has shown that "specific and teachable communication behaviors" can be attributed to reducing malpractice claims. Why? Because we routinely interact with others during volatile times in their lives. These occasions merit the type of thoughtful communication highlighted in the coming pages.

In summary, the focus of this text is to help you understand how the human mind works following an emergency. Many of the people with whom you come into contact will be suffering from physical and psychological injury. Your awareness to this reality – as well as your recollection of core concepts covered in this text – will improve the quality of these experiences for everyone involved and increase your effectiveness as an emergency responder!

Jeffrey S. Katz,
Lieutenant, Boynton Beach Police Department  www.bbpd.org
Doctoral Student, Walden University USA  www.waldenu.edu

## Tips to Help You Integrate These Skills

### Setting up your brain for new information

This Handbook uses accelerated learning techniques. To get the most from this material, consider the following ideas.

A **Table of Contents** is a <u>linear</u> display of what to expect. That's normal, but what's much better is a graphical representation of that same information. Why? Since over 80% of your mental processing is visual, your brain loves pictures. The Table of Contents can be transformed into a Concept Map. Just the act of creating a map of a book's contents sets up *file folders* in your mind where information goes when you actually read it.

On the page to the right, there is a concept map of this Handbook. You will see it again at the start of each chapter. Make your own Concept Map on a large piece of paper so that you can add notes to it as you read along.

**The Index** - Before you begin to read a book, examine the index. Highlight any terms that have multiple references because they must be important. This book's Index is on pages 78-79.

**Review** - If you're the first to go down a hill in a toboggan after a snowfall, it might be slow-going. Someone following in your track will go a bit faster - and the next run will be even faster. It is the same principle when learning new material. To have it integrated and planted in your permanent memory for later recall, you need to toboggan down that hill a few times. That is done through review. As you explore this material, make notes on your own Concept Map so that you can use it as a review source.

We have also provided a couple of review exercises beginning on page 58. Enhance your experience by doing these exercises with a colleague.

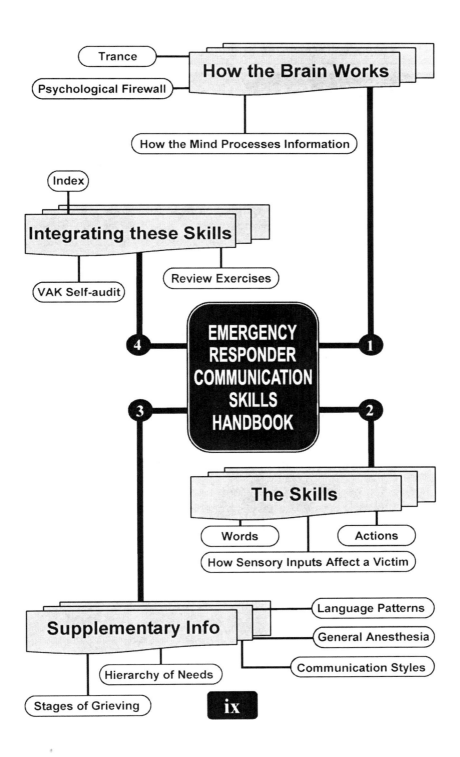

Trance

Psychological Firewall

**How the Brain Works**

How the Mind Processes Information

Index

**Integrating these Skills**

Review Exercises

VAK Self-audit

**4**

**EMERGENCY RESPONDER COMMUNICATION SKILLS HANDBOOK**

**1**

**3**

**2**

**The Skills**

Words

Actions

How Sensory Inputs Affect a Victim

Language Patterns

General Anesthesia

**Supplementary Info**

Communication Styles

Hierarchy of Needs

Stages of Grieving

ix

# Introduction

## Clear communication enhances safety for both the victim and the responder

As a professional responding to a medical emergency, your ability to appropriately communicate with a casualty is as vital as your skill in rendering aid. Your words, your actions, and the surrounding environment can crucially influence the victim and the outcome.

Your experience has taught you that stress can disrupt clear thinking, scramble short-term memory, and effectively sabotage interpersonal communication.

Skills described in this book will apply in many emergencies. You will probably find them less useful for people disoriented by drugs. As always, use your own judgement.

If you are responsible for the care and welfare of others in any aspect of your work, these concepts and techniques are for you.

Although this book is written for **police officers, paramedics, and firefighters, it can also be valuable for rescue workers.**

Due to the importance of communication skills, more and more medical schools have, over the past decade, added this subject to their curricula.

These innovative techniques are learnable. This book is meant to complement and enhance the hard skills you use daily on the job.

*Brian Walsh*

# How the brain works
## The foundation for the rest of the book

| | |
|---|---|
| Set up for this Chapter | 3 |
| How the Mind Processes Information | 4 |
| Psychological Firewall | 10 |
| Trance | 14 |

# How your words and actions can support patient comfort and survival

| | |
|---|---|
| Set up for this Chapter | 19 |
| How Your Actions Affect an Injured Person | 20 |
| How Your Words Affect an Injured Person | 24 |
| How Sensory Inputs Affect an Injured Person | 36 |

# Supplementary Information
## "Nice to Know"

| | |
|---|---|
| General Anesthesia and the Subconscious Mind | 42 |
| Maslow's Hierarchy of Needs | 44 |
| Communication Styles | 46 |
| The Stages of Grieving | 52 |
| Language Patterns and Embedded Commands | 53 |

# Integrating these Skills

| | |
|---|---|
| Review Exercises | 58 |
| VAK Self-Audit | 63 |
| Index | 78 |

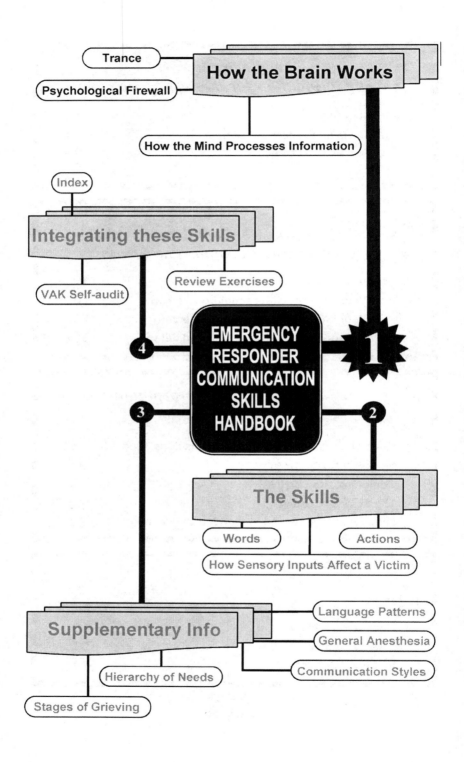

Trance

Psychological Firewall

How the Brain Works

How the Mind Processes Information

Index

Integrating these Skills

VAK Self-audit

Review Exercises

EMERGENCY
RESPONDER
COMMUNICATION
SKILLS
HANDBOOK

4

3

2

1

The Skills

Words

Actions

How Sensory Inputs Affect a Victim

Supplementary Info

Language Patterns

General Anesthesia

Communication Styles

Hierarchy of Needs

Stages of Grieving

# 1

# How The Brain Works

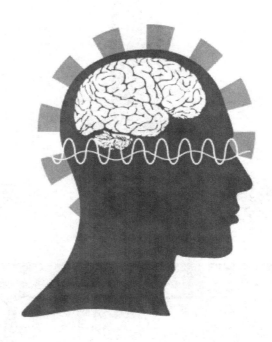

## *Let me set up Chapter 1 . . .*

This chapter is the foundation for Chapter 2.

Here we will explore how information gathered by the senses is processed by the brain. I will explain the differences between the Conscious and Subconscious Minds. This will help you understand why a specific event can cause a range of reactions.

**It is really important to understand that when someone experiences sudden agitation or stress (accident, injury, trauma, or serious threat), this person immediately goes into an altered state of consciousness. In effect, this is a trance, not unlike being in a hypnotic or daydream state.**

This condition is typically accompanied by several psychological and physiological manifestations that you may or may not be aware of.

This Handbook focuses on a casualty's emotional and psychological states. Chapter 2 will give you some unique ways to communicate with those under your care.

# How the Mind Processes Information

The best definition of the mind I know is
by Professor Daniel J. Siegel MD of UCLA:

> *The mind is a process that regulates the flow of energy and information*

At this juncture, it is crucial for you to understand the difference between your *Conscious* and *Subconscious Minds*. **This will help you master the skills offered in this Handbook.**

**Your <u>awareness of your thoughts and experiences</u> is your Conscious Mind, also called the Thinking Mind.**

That just means you are attentive to what is going on in and around you. Although some of this activity involves you directly, some of it is just what you are observing in real time. It also includes what you are remembering, imagining, and visualizing.

You probably believe that as you see, hear, touch, smell, and taste something, you become aware of it immediately. In fact, that's not so. When your senses take in new information, it is analyzed and evaluated through an array of complex emotional, perceptual, prejudicial, and defensive filters. Then, and only then, will some of that information become available for your <u>conscious</u> awareness and deliberate processing. This happens in a split second, but it does happen.

This is significant. Just read on and I'll explain why as I lay the foundation for everything that you'll learn in this book.

## Let's discuss the characteristics of the Conscious and Subconscious Minds.

If you were to place your feet flat on the floor, the area under your feet represents the power and potential of your <u>Conscious Mind</u>. The area in the rest of the room symbolizes the power and resources of your <u>Subconscious Mind</u>, and this is where the action is.

## The Conscious Mind

Since most people are more familiar with their Conscious Mind, I'll explain this first. Your Conscious Mind is what you are aware of <u>right at this very moment</u>. In reality, you can hold only one conscious thought at a time.

### We are not born with a Conscious Mind.

Our Conscious Mind begins to develop at about the age of two and is entirely in place by the age of seven to ten. Remember this bit of information as I will come back to it later.

**There are four sets of attributes of the Conscious Mind.**

**1** ### LINEAR, LOGICAL, ANALYTICAL

The first set of characteristics of the Conscious Mind is that it is *Linear, Logical,* and *Analytical.* It works in details, thrives on orderliness, and is stubborn.

When we say that someone is thinking inside the box - that's what we mean. Way too much in the head, and not enough confidence in gut intuition. These traits are useful in some situations, but not so helpful in others.

**2** ### TEMPORARY MEMORY

The second feature is like the RAM in your computer – it is short-term storage that enables processing and facilitation. It's what allows you to follow a story, or keep track of a conversation.

> *Many years ago, as a clinical hypnotherapist, I ran smoking cessation workshops.*
>
> *A question I would ask the group as we began each session was who had previously attempted to stop the habit.*
>
> *Regardless of the conscious method used (patch, gum, whatever)* ***Willpower*** *was involved.*

**3** ### WILLPOWER

This facet is generally quite unreliable and frail. Why is willpower so unreliable? Simply because it is influenced by the final aspect of the Conscious Mind (Rationalization).

# 4 RATIONALIZATION

Rationalization means making excuses. We justify all sorts of actions daily, don't we? "Oh, just one more piece of pie – that's not going to hurt." Can you appreciate how our willpower is consciously compromised?

> *The mind is like an iceberg. It floats*
> *with one-seventh of its bulk above water.*
> Dr. Sigmund Freud

# The Subconscious Mind

Also known as the Non-conscious or Unconscious Mind, it is everything that is going on in your mind that you are not aware of right now. There are three main characteristics here.

## 1 PERMANENT MEMORY

For anything to be stored in the Permanent Memory, it must be filtered, analyzed, deemed important enough to keep, and then encoded for long-term storage. It has lots of hoops to jump through, but there are good reasons for that. You are flooded with so much information, your mind must be discrete in selecting what is actually stored.

If I asked you for your home phone number, you'd probably be able to tell me immediately. It was not in your conscious mind before I asked you, was it? No - It was stored in the *Permanent Memory*, part of your Subconscious Mind.

Storage of information into the permanent memory of the Subconscious Mind is automatic if it has any <u>emotion</u> attached to it, or if it has anything to do with <u>survival</u>.

Think back to the first memory you can recall from your childhood. Chances are it involves an emotion or a scary episode, maybe both. Was it your fifth birthday party? Perhaps getting punished by your teacher? Perhaps a win or loss at a sports competition?

**2   <u>EMOTIONS AND PATTERNS (HABITS)</u>**

*Emotions* and *patterns* are located in the Subconscious Mind. The Subconscious Mind is a very powerful servant that follows instructions to the letter. Like a computer program, it will continue to operate in a set pattern (good or bad) until it is given new instructions. The Subconscious Mind is an extraordinary *multitasker.*

NICE TO KNOW

**Maladaptive behaviors and limiting beliefs**

Many mental-health therapists agree that most patterns begin in childhood, often before the age of seven. This period of personality development is known as the *Imprint Phase.*

*Does the name Pavlov ring a bell?*

On pages 10 and 12, I explain why young children are so impressionable

8

## 3  PROTECTION & SELF-PRESERVATION (SURVIVAL)

If the Subconscious Mind detects danger, it activates the fight-or-flight response. Aside from a host of physical reactions, we may find ourselves behaving in uncharacteristic ways. These are triggered by defense responses that are either innate or acquired in our childhood.

The next few pages will show you how we acquire these defensive patterns when we're young.

## Characteristics of Our Minds

| CONSCIOUS | SUBCONSCIOUS |
|---|---|
| Holds single thought only | Always multitasking |
| Active and controlling | Receptive, participatory |
| Deeper into detail  (Analytical) | Considers the big picture |
| Competitive | Collaborative |
| External | Internal |
| From parts to whole | From whole to parts |
| Responds figuratively | Responds literally |
| Objective | Subjective |
| Obsessed with correctness | Takes path of least resistance |
| Rational and Logical | Irrational |
| Serial and Linear | Parallel and seeks links |
| Specific | Ambiguous |
| Temporary Memory | Permanent Memory |
| Thoughtful | Emotional |
| Willpower | Habits and Patterns |

# Psychological Firewall

Additional protection is provided by a type of psychological firewall known as the **Critical Faculty.** Like the Conscious Mind, it begins to develop at about the age of two, and is fully functional by seven or eight.

Like a gatekeeper, it prevents suggestions from *imprinting* the impressionable Subconscious Mind. Since young children do not have this protective shield, they are highly influenced by suggestions (good or bad). See more of this on page 12.

## Adults can also be imprinted

The Critical Faculty is mentioned often in this Handbook. It is essential that you understand the concept. Here are a couple of examples.

The advertising folks appreciate that emotions are the key to getting people to buy something.

Emotions are in the Subconscious Mind, and the Ad folks are well aware of the Critical Faculty.

When evaluating the potential of a new advertisement, they rate its *CFB (Critical Faculty Bypass).*

## *Imagine this:*

You're sitting down in front of your TV. An advertisement comes on.

A salesman is standing in front of a lot full of cars.

*There has never been a better time to...*
### buy a car on Saturday.
*We've sharpened our pencils, and we're willing to talk. We'll have hot dogs for the kids...*

As he is giving you his sales pitch, over his shoulder at the back of the lot, you notice someone dressed in a very bright yellow chicken suit – waving its wings.

Your conscious attention is drawn to the Chicken-man and you no longer listen to the sales pitch. *Or do you?*

What happens in that moment is CFB, Critical Faculty Bypass. In this state, your Conscious Mind is being tricked into focusing on the Chicken-Man - leaving your Subconscious Mind to receive the sales pitch as a potent suggestion.

**Somehow... on Saturday...**
**you have this inclination to visit the car salesman!**

11

We must be very careful what we say in front of youngsters. Everything heard, seen, or witnessed is imprinted in their permanent memory, and is accepted as the gospel truth - and all of this plays a part in shaping the child's beliefs, attitudes, and behaviors.

Children trust the wisdom and life experience of their caretakers. In effect, a child's perception is:

**Your ideas = My reality**

| Adult Statement | If heard before age of 7-10 | Hearing it with Critical Faculty in place |
|---|---|---|
| You're stupid. It's a good thing you're cute, because you're not very smart. | **Accepted as truth** | **Has little or no impact** |
| Your room is so messy. You'll never amount to anything in this world. | **Shapes behaviors** | |
| You just don't get it. How dumb can you be? | **& beliefs** | |

**Another way that Critical Faculty Bypass can occur is when someone goes into trance.**

**Understanding trance is key to how your actions and words influence the victim's outcome.**

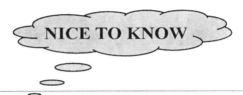

NICE TO KNOW

Trance is often associated with formal hypnotic induction. Other ways to induce trance are shown on the next page.

A client might want to stop
- unwanted behaviors or attitudes
- smoking
- grinding teeth
- nail biting
- self-sabotage

To effect change, a hypnotherapist needs to bypass the Critical Faculty in order to reach the Subconscious Mind where all the patterns and emotions reside.

To do this, a client is guided into a hypnotic trance. How does a hypnotherapist guide a client into trance?

He or she generally uses a combination of focused attention, progressive relaxation, and/or confusion. There are other ways that trance can be achieved. Read on…

# Trance

A person can drift into trance through repetitive beats (dancing, chanting, drumming), monotony, disorientation, confusion, stimulus overload, pain, meditation, massage, and even sudden fright, alarm, or panic.

Everyone experiences trance differently. Some may appear lucid, drowsy, in a daydream, even unconscious.

The important thing to remember is...

### *When people are in trance, their Critical Faculty is bypassed.*

### *Anything they hear goes directly into their Subconscious Mind as a suggestion to follow.*

**As an emergency responder, you'll constantly be in situations that put people into trance**

- ◆ Graphic and gory scenes
- ◆ Severe pain
- ◆ Physical or emotional abuse
- ◆ Trauma
- ◆ Drug use
- ◆ Intense fear
- ◆ Shock
- ◆ Chronic discomfort
- ◆ Being unconscious
- ◆ Natural disasters
- ◆ Explosions
- ◆ Involvement in or witnessing accidents
- ◆ Involvement in or witnessing fights, conflict, or aggression

In trance, senses are highly acute. Hearing, sight, smell, and taste are magnified. Anything picked up by peripheral vision also bypasses the Critical Faculty and channeled directly to the Subconscious Mind.

**All the above applies even if the victim is unconscious.**

*Treat and talk to unconscious casualties*
*as if they are conscious.*

If someone in the crowd says:

*"Look at all that blood - He's not going to make it."*

That utterance can go directly into the victim's Subconscious Mind affecting chances for survival.

*Let me be clear . . .*

This **does not** mean that this utterance will severely impact your patient's recovery. It simply means that this one small nudge could tip the balance against a natural recovery.

This is your golden opportunity to use the tools, tips, and techniques in this Handbook to offset careless talk that may affect your patient.

Chapter 2 provides you with knowledge about why these tools work and how best to employ them.

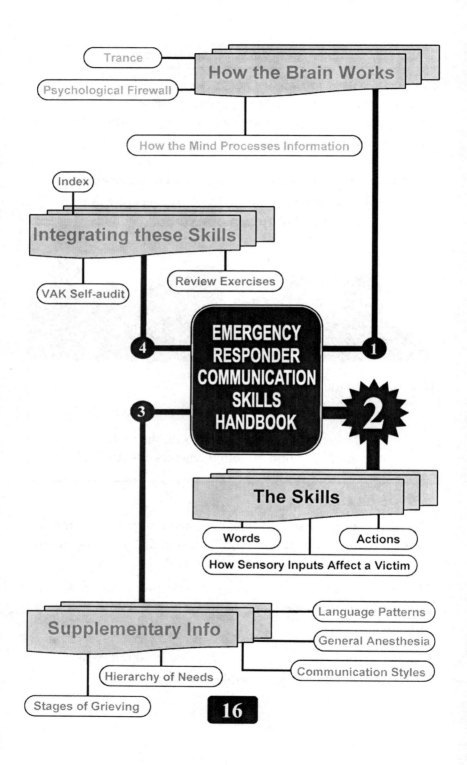

Trance

Psychological Firewall

How the Brain Works

How the Mind Processes Information

Index

Integrating these Skills

VAK Self-audit

Review Exercises

4

EMERGENCY RESPONDER COMMUNICATION SKILLS HANDBOOK

1

3

2

The Skills

Words

Actions

How Sensory Inputs Affect a Victim

Supplementary Info

Language Patterns

General Anesthesia

Communication Styles

Hierarchy of Needs

Stages of Grieving

# 2

## Actions
## Words
## Senses

*The art of communication
is the language of leadership*

James C. Humes

*Words represent your intellect.*

*The sound, gestures,
and movement
represent your feelings.*

Patricia Fripp

*Words are, of course,
the most powerful drug
used by mankind.*

Rudyard Kipling

*Things that upset a terrier
may pass virtually unnoticed
by a Great Dane.*

Smiley Blanton

18

*Let me set up Chapter 2 . . .*

In an emergency, patients are likely in trance, What you **say** and **do** is just as critical as the medical attention you give them.

They could be anywhere from unconscious to highly unfocused or highly obsessed. Employing the communications skills found in this Handbook, you can help them focus on what is beneficial to relieve discomfort and enable recovery.

Other than their injuries and pain, many factors affect victims during an emergency. We'll discuss:

◆ How Your Actions Affect Your Patient
◆ How Your Words Affect Your Patient
◆ How Sensory Inputs Affect Your Patient

A patient in an agitated emotional state may be in a light hyper-suggestible trance. This means that words have the power to go directly into the Subconscious Mind as directions to be followed.

*This effect is magnified when the attending person is in uniform.*

**IMPORTANT NOTE**

When people are unconscious, their Subconscious Mind is <u>still on high alert</u> and takes in everything going on around them.

*Treat and talk to unconscious patients as if they are conscious.*

19

# How Your Actions Affect an Injured Person

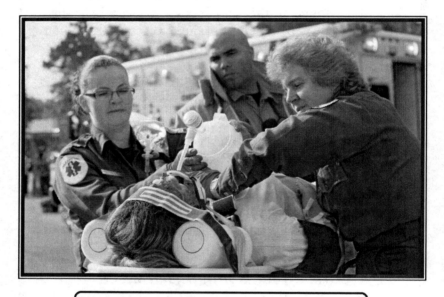

*The most important thing you wear is the expression on your face.*

Anonymous

**You have just come in contact with a distressed person.** Assume that his or her Critical Faculty has been bypassed, and you are being acutely observed by the patient's Subconscious Mind. Employ these actions as best you can.

- When you see victims for the first time, be aware of your facial expressions. Avoid outward expressions of any shock you may be feeling. Ensure your facial expressions exude calmness and a sense of confidence that everything is OK.

- Approach them with a calm manner and clear voice.

- Consider removing mirrored sunglasses or a pervasive hat. Face-to face communication is improved when you can see into each other's eyes.

- Avoid standing over them – move down to their eye level and look them in the eyes if you can (only if it is culturally appropriate). If you are facing them with the sun or bright lights behind you, you'll appear as a shadow. That's not good. A faceless voice is unsettling, so let them see you.

- For a moment, touch their shoulder, forehead, or hold their hand while reassuring them or giving instructions. Human touch is comforting and calming for most people. You are their lifeline. Again, only if this is culturally appropriate.

- As you are aware, there are many medical benefits to covering a patient with a blanket. For most people, being covered is a comfort and can lower anxiety. Be aware that some people might have a negative psychological association with being covered.

- Ensure that their sight and hearing are not impeded. Stress is often a result of people's perception of their lack of control. Check that their eyes are not covered or ears blocked. Make sure no bright lights shine directly into their eyes.

- Include them in your actions where possible: Tell them what you're doing. If family or friends are close by, include them to decrease any general anxiety.

At the beginning of this Handbook, I illustrated the power of the Subconscious Mind by using the *feet on the floor* analogy. Here's another good example: Think of the Subconscious Mind as the 85% of an iceberg that is hidden under the water's surface.

One distinct resource of the Subconscious Mind is the ability to detect subtle physical cues (body language) that are generally beyond the awareness of either party.

Our words are important. However, a great deal of communication is largely <u>non</u>-verbal, and most of this is not in our own conscious awareness. Non-verbal cues include voice cadence and tone, hand motions, gestures, facial expressions, and posture. Most of these are picked up by the Subconscious Mind.

Non-verbal cues often contradict our words. As such, the **Subconscious Mind gives more value to non-verbal cues**. Ensure that your body language does not betray any doubts about a victim's potential for a full recovery.

Always display an air of confidence.

---

*When the eyes say one thing, and the tongue another,*
*a practiced man relies on the language of the <u>first</u>.*
Ralph Waldo Emerson

---

On the next page, I've listed some body language attributes for most Western cultures, that can positively or negatively impact outcomes.
**Please note that some other cultures**
**do not welcome touching or direct eye contact.**

22

| BODY LANGUAGE | | |
| --- | --- | --- |
| | UNHELPFUL | HELPFUL |
| Gestures | Clenching hands, jiggling foot, rubbing hair or back of your neck, Touching your face. | Leaning forward Using gentle, engaging hand gestures |
| Eyes | Avoiding eye contact Looking down Nervously looking away or side-to-side Non-smiling eyes | Getting down to their level Looking them in the eyes. Being open and honest |
| Posture | Leaning back, arms folded, legs crossed, stooped, rigid body | Being relaxed, upright, and confident |
| Facial | Showing disinterest or disagreement | Showing sincerity and interest Matching what they say |
| Head | Shaking (side-to-side) shows disapproval | Nodding shows approval Tilting shows that you're listening |

23

# How Your Words Affect an Injured Person

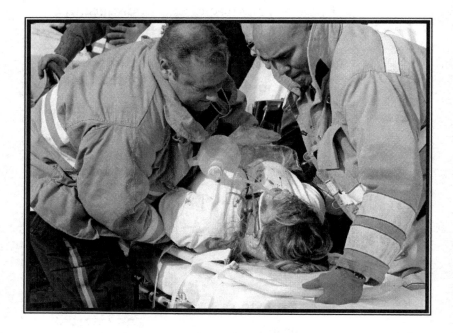

*The difference between the right word*
*and the __almost__ right word*
*is the difference between*
*lightning and a lightning bug.*

Mark Twain

The next few pages will give you plenty of ideas on how to best use words with your patient. Here is just a teaser to start.

| INSTEAD OF THIS | SAY THIS |
|---|---|
| A little bee sting. *(no such thing)* | Some people feel this; some people don't. |
| Looks like that must hurt a lot. | Let me know where you ... feel any discomfort. |
| Do you feel like vomiting? | How does your tummy feel? |
| Are you feeling better? | You look/sound like... you are feeling better. |
| See if this Nitroglycerin tablet (spray) will help. | Take this. It will make you... feel more comfortable. |
| Has the oxygen helped your breathing? | The oxygen has really helped your breathing. You're looking better already. |
| Oops! | Let me just do that again. |

## The "YES" Set

A common technique in the sales industry is to state two or three truths to a client. Then follow up with a final phrase that may be believed as truthful.

When dealing with a patient, you can say:
1. *As you lie there,*
2. *listening to the sound of my voice,*
3. *you can now begin to relax, knowing things are fine.*

**These tips have been collected from a number of your colleagues. Some may seem like common sense, yet in the field, immediate tasks often trump good communication.**

- Look them in the eyes - if culturally appropriate.

- Use their name. One of the most comforting things that people can hear is their own name. This helps them to feel grounded.

- Introduce yourself.

- Speak calmly and confidently.

- Be sincere. Let them know you care about them.

- Speak quietly and close to their ear. Use a natural tone, volume, pitch, and pace.

- Reassure your patient that you will address any pain as quickly as possible.

- Avoid nervously clearing your throat, or saying "um, uh."

- Use plain language. Avoid very complex sentences or technical jargon.

- If you need to discuss your patient's condition, step out of earshot of the victim, family, or bystanders.

- Allow the patient to express any concerns, anxieties, fears, or anger.

- Allow the patient to ask questions.

- If a patient is obsessed or frightened, a way to settle him or her is to say: ***Focus on your breathing.***

- It is easy to misunderstand what is said in haste.
  - ▶ To check the accuracy of your understanding of what was said, paraphrase what you hear back to your patient.
  - ▶ To verify that the patient understood your explanation and instructions, repeat and summarize important information. Ask them to state their understanding of what you said.

- It's important that patients hold a positive image of the future. Ask them about their family, their vacation plans, or whatever. Have them focus on something to look forward to and the good things in life.

- Use phrases like:
  *That will be more comfortable*
  *That looks better          That sounds better*
  *That's good                You're doing a good job*

- Tell them that once they reach the hospital, someone will ask them for a contact name of a friend or family member. This will give them one more thing to look forward to and may somewhat reduce their anxiety.

- Keep talking to your patients. Tell them what you are doing, what they will hear or feel.
  *Janice, I'm going to make sure you are secured to the board now. You'll hear the sound of the Velcro and then you will feel me snug you up so know you are safe and secure. Legs first, here we go...*

27

## Negative Words are Counter-productive

Research has shown that it is 30% more difficult to understand a negative statement or question than it is a positive one. Since patients are already in a fragile condition, make it as easy as possible by using positive statements.

Most mental processing is <u>visual</u>, so the most functional words are those that evoke an image. Copywriters, especially in the advertising industry, know this. The Subconscious Mind does its best to make a picture out of everything it hears. Sometimes that is impossible.

Here is the enigma about negative words. You **cannot** **not** think about something without first thinking about it.

If I asked you NOT to think about a giraffe in a pink tutu, it would be virtually impossible for you <u>not</u> to think about it unless you thought about it first. The mind has to make an image of that giraffe <u>before</u> it can follow the instruction <u>not</u> to think about it.

If someone, in an attempt to change a pattern, says the phrase: "I <u>don't</u> like chocolate cake." – the Subconscious Mind makes a picture for every word **except: "don't."**

The result is the exact opposite to what was intended:
"I ≈ like chocolate cake."

*If you Google* **NO CLOCKS** - *What will you get?*

---

**When consoling someone, avoid negative words.**

On the next page are some examples of negative phrases and how they might be reworded.

---

| INSTEAD OF SAYING | SAY THIS |
|---|---|
| Don't worry. | Rest assured that… |
| You're not going to die. | You're going to live. |
| Sit here on the stretcher where my hand is and don't slide down. | Sit here on the stretcher where my hand is and stay right in that spot. |
| Don't talk like that. | I understand what you mean. |
| Don't be so depressed. | Things will get better. |
| Don't give up. | Focus all your energy on your healing. |
| This isn't going to hurt. | As I apply this bandage, you might feel a slightly cool pressure. |
| Your problems aren't that big. | Everything is cool. |
| Don't be afraid. | We are well trained to take care of you. |
| It's not that bad. | This is a lot better than you might think. |
| Don't feel sad. Don't be so down. | You'll be feeling better very soon. |
| Things aren't that bad. | Things are well in hand. |
| I'm not going to leave you. | I will stay right with you. |
| No problem. No worries. | Things are better than they may seem. You're safe now. You are in better shape than you may think. |

# Direct & Indirect Language Patterns

Many psychotherapists use two very distinct language patterns. <u>Each has its place</u> because, while everyone uses both direct and indirect language patterns, some people may favor one over the other. Therefore, I want you to appreciate their respective strengths and weaknesses.

## Indirect Patterns

**Indirect Language** is characteristically vague and leaves room for wide interpretation. Typically, a speaker implies something and expects the listener to deduce the correct message. Common examples are sarcasm and irony.

Guess what? It does not always work that way. For instance, a young physician might be reluctant to instruct an older patient to reduce weight. So, the physician skirts around the issue by dropping hints as to a course of action. Most people do not correctly interpret these kinds of indirect messages.

> *The notion of implied meaning*
> *is the root of misunderstanding.*
> Eric Parslow

See page 53 for some imaginative ways to use Indirect Language Patterns.

## Direct Patterns

**Direct language** gets right to the point and leaves no room for misunderstanding.

When you're dealing with an injured person, you are giving vital instructions. Be clear by using direct language patterns when compliance is required.

A health-care professional, when giving directions to a patient or a colleague, would be wise to use direct language patterns to ensure understanding and compliance.

**Giving your casualties a task to do will distract them from their discomfort and anxiety. For example:**

> ♦   *Susan - Take slow deep breaths.*
>      *It will help you be more comfortable.*
>
> ♦   *Mike - Hold this dressing on your hand*
>      *so that I can check your legs.*
>
> ♦   *Janice - I am about to proceed with the*
>      *intravenous. I want you to wiggle your toes.*
>
> ♦   *Blair - Hold this oxygen mask to your face*
>      *and breathe normally.*

Some emergency responders have small stuffed animals in their vehicles. Children handed the new toy are asked to give it a name. The impact this has on an injured or scared child is highly visible.

## A Beneficial White Lie

One excellent method to instill a belief of a positive outcome is to tell, or agree with, a small untruth. This can offset fear, pain, or panic, and generate hope. The patient gains a degree of control. Remember, a patient's greater sense of control means less anxiety and stress.

Keep your language positive, supportive, and real. If what you say is unrealistic, you will begin to damage the rapport you have already established.

On the other hand, if the patient expresses these hopeful thoughts, here is a wonderful opportunity to be genuinely supportive. Do more than just nod your head – build on what the patient says - express agreement.

The patient might say for example:

- ◆ I'm going to make it, right?
- ◆ I'm OK right?
- ◆ I'll still be able to play sports, right?
- ◆ I'll be able to play my piano again, right?
- ◆ Is my car alright?
- ◆ I'll be able to see my family soon, right?

## Lighten Up

Once the injured person is stabilized and convinced that you understand his or her predicament, it might help to use some minor and subtle humor.

This might help the patient believe the situation isn't as bad as once imagined. Here are some examples of phrases you could use:

- ♦ I bet there are a lot of places you'd rather be right now.
- ♦ A few weeks from now, you'll look back at this and laugh.
- ♦ You'll have a good story to tell your family and friends.
- ♦ Are we having fun yet?
- ♦ It could have been worse—you might have ...

| *Do you have a few of your own?* |
|---|
|  |
|  |
|  |
|  |
|  |
|  |

## The Stanton Communications Checklist

This checklist was developed by Jim Stanton of Stanton Associates, a firm that specializes in emergency preparedness and crisis communications. © 2010 Stanton Associates

**In times of uncertainty, victims and their families are disoriented and confused, but their anxiety can be reduced as and when they become aware of essential facts. As a professional, you have a duty to facilitate the flow of vital information. The questions in the following checklist are asked from the perspective of victims or their family members.**

### What is really happening?

Saying nothing to them allows their imagination to run wild. See page 37 about Awfulizing or Catastrophizing. You don't have to go into detail. Just give them enough information to quell their fear. You also need to understand that rumors will abound, and that you need to provide facts in order to circumvent that from happening. Be truthful and kind; and focus on the positive.

### How will this affect me?

A standard marketing approach is WIIFM (What's in it for me?). You will be making decisions about what will happen next, and about how, when, and where it will happen. By sharing with them how the next step will help, in their eyes you will be more a savior than just someone doing a job. Be aware that "Me" also means "My" and that the victim is not only worried about self, but also family, children in school, elderly parents, partners out of town on business or working at another location, and even pets.

One exception to this approach is in the case of rape. Victims need to feel that they have a sense of control and a say in their recovery.

### What are you doing?

Again, you will want to avoid details, but keeping them in the loop will thwart bizarre assumptions. You need to make sure they know you are a first responder, what "brand" you are (paramedic, police officer, firefighter, etc.) and what you are doing, or about to do.

## What do I need to do?

Giving them specific direct instructions will distract their attention from the pain or injury. If you have nothing better to say, you can always revert to the old standard: "Focus on your breathing" instruction, and thus promote homeostasis. Remember this is a very traumatic and frightening time for them, so be reassuring and calming. Branding helps, so tell them the emergency service you represent.

## Specific and detailed instructions.

Remember that when under stress, people are in a trance, and they are just not thinking clearly. A good practice is to repeat your directions more than once. Keep your instructions simple and avoid jargon like airways, EOC, and the like.

If you deal with someone who has difficulty following your <u>verbal</u> directions, it may be that he or she has low auditory abilities. One approach is to use <u>visual</u> cues. For example, look them in the eyes and demonstrate deep breathing. Then point and nod to them to follow. See page 49.

## When will things get back to normal?

Their world has been turned upside down. Be honest, yet positive. You may have to be vague by simply saying that you have seen many situations like this and even though the next few days may be troublesome, the outlook for them is good. Tell them what you know and if you don't have an answer, tell them that as well. Give them a specific task to complete. such as, "If you have ongoing health issues, consult your family physician." You can also refer them to a help-point such as a website or toll-free number.

## Reassurance.

Even basic first aid courses teach this concept. You can be sure that when you reassure and encourage your patients it will generate positive expectation in their Subconscious Minds, and help enhance healing. People have great trust in first responders, and look to you for direction and guidance. Build on that trust.

# How Sensory Inputs Affect an Injured Person

*The best cure for the body is a quiet mind.*

Napoléon Bonaparte

36

## How To Ease Your Patients' Feelings of Vulnerability, Distress, Pain, and Fear

You have the power to improve your patients' situations. Your calming demeanor, intentional words, and your actions can significantly lessen the impact on their already magnified senses.

Traumatized people are usually in trance and often do not know how seriously they are injured. Their active imagination can magnify everything they hear, see, smell, taste, and feel.

Psychology terms for this are *Awfulizing* or *Catastrophizing:* Believing that something is far worse than it actually is.

Remember, injured persons may be in trance with their Critical Faculty bypassed and sensory inputs greatly magnified.

If someone in the crowd says:

> *"Look at the car - Nobody can survive that."*

This can go directly into the victim's Subconscious Mind as a negative suggestion, possibly compromising chances for recovery. One more good reason to keep the crowd back!

## Sensory inputs that have the potential to increase anxiety

- Sight of blood (whether their own or someone else's).

- Loud or unfamiliar noises. If safe to do so, ensure sirens and emergency flashing lights are off or minimized to reduce stress on your patient.

- Sight or smell of smoke.

- Shouting, nervous tremors in your voice.

- Comments from people close by.
  (*or even farther away - remember their hearing is magnified*)

- The looks on people's faces, especially yours.

- The taste of blood, vomit, bile, etc.

- Feeling cold, hot, or damp.

- Feeling pain due to position or injury.

- Being partially or fully naked.

- The presence of non-essential personnel, such bystanders, some family members, superfluous emergency responders.

## Position Changes

If you are ready to reposition or move your patient to make him or her more comfortable or to improve circulation, you may wish to use any of the following phrases:

- Will you be more comfortable if…?
- You'll notice, as I move your arm, how much better you'll feel.
- That looks more comfortable.
- Much more comfortable, isn't it? - Sure it is.

**Here are a few suggestions to assist you in  neutralizing the surrounding stimuli.**

Do as many as you can.  The calmer your patients are, the easier they are to care for, and the better their chance for a quick recovery. Your specific circumstances will dictate what you can or cannot do.

---

- ◆ Move bystanders far away.

- ◆ If possible, move your patient away from the accident scene.

- ◆ Cool or warm the patient as appropriate.

- ◆ Move your patient to a quieter, less public spot.

- ◆ Wipe mud, blood, and debris from their face especially, ears, eyes, and nose.

- ◆ Cover a patient who has had clothing removed.

- ◆ Always keep your patients' comfort in mind. If possible, position their body so they can be more comfortable (arms stretched overhead, pinned underneath them, or hanging off stretchers is not comfortable) If you wouldn't be comfortable in that position, they probably aren't either.

---

**Remember - Talk to and treat an <u>unconscious</u> person the same as a <u>conscious</u> one. His or her Subconscious Mind is on high alert, monitoring everything you say and do.**

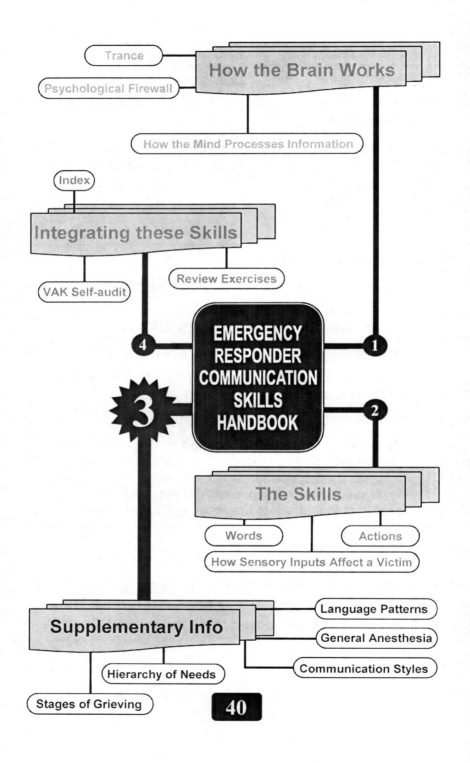

Trance

Psychological Firewall

How the Brain Works

How the Mind Processes Information

Index

Integrating these Skills

VAK Self-audit

Review Exercises

4

EMERGENCY
RESPONDER
COMMUNICATION
SKILLS
HANDBOOK

1

3

2

The Skills

Words

Actions

How Sensory Inputs Affect a Victim

Supplementary Info

Language Patterns

General Anesthesia

Communication Styles

Hierarchy of Needs

Stages of Grieving

# Supplementary Information

## "Nice to Know"

# General Anesthesia and the Subconscious Mind

## Can a patient under a general anesthetic remember what the surgical team discussed? Well, yes and no.

A great deal of formal research and anecdotal evidence has produced <u>mixed</u> results. Why? Simply because researchers measured the wrong thing. They focused on what was remembered by the <u>Conscious Mind</u>. Interesting, but not useful.

### In the context of this Handbook...
### what is most relevant is the impact that
### words can have on the patient's prospects of recovery.

Following a gallbladder removal, the patient experienced severe pain of an unexplained nature. A battery of tests revealed no physiological basis for this. In hypnosis, the patient was able to repeat verbatim what was said by the surgical team. **One phrase in particular was relevant.**

After making the incision and exposing the gallbladder, the surgeon said: **"Take a look at that gallbladder! She'll never be the same after this."** Obviously, the patient's Subconscious Mind inferred that this was bad news.

When subsequently questioned, the surgeon admitted that he was actually expressing <u>how well</u> he expected the operation to go because her condition was not as serious as previously diagnosed. Once the patient's Subconscious Mind became aware of this, the pain quickly vanished.

If you would like to know more, here are just a few examples of this research:

- ◆ *Parahypnosis: Unconscious Perception Under Chemoanesthesia* May 1969 Journal of the National Medical Association (Vol. 61, # 3 pp 246-247)
- ◆ *Awareness During General Anaesthesia* March 1972 Canadian Journal of Anesthesia (Vol. 19, # 2)
- ◆ *Information-processing under general anaesthesia: a review* April 1988 Journal of The Royal Society of Medicine (81-4: pp 224-227)
- ◆ *Conscious awareness during general anaesthesia: patients' perceptions, emotions, cognition and reactions* 1998 British Journal of Anaesthesia (80: pp 133-139)

**As outlined earlier, patients' Subconscious Minds cannot ignore comments that pertain to their survival.**

Remember, the Subconscious Mind interprets and responds to information *literally*. Vague, careless remarks can be misunderstood by the Subconscious Mind and thus contribute to slower recovery and post-operative pain and suffering.

**These following remarks may negatively impact a patient's recovery:**

- Just a moment! I don't like the patient's color.
- The tube is too big, but - we don't have another.
- This woman is lost anyhow.
- She needs more anesthetic.
- How can a man be so fat?
- There's a lot of blood loss here.

It is vital that conversations in the operating room be positive. Medical staff should understand that a patient's Subconscious Mind vigilantly monitors their chatter: be it positive or negative.

The use of positive suggestions during, or shortly following, general anesthesia has proven to decrease the duration of post-op hospitalization and reduce pain and suffering. For example:

- You are now going into a deep state of relaxation. Breathe slowly and deeply. With each breath you take, you will feel yourself going deeper and deeper relaxed. That's right. Good. So relaxed.
- As expected, everything is going just fine.
- You did great. A wonderful result.
- When you return to full awareness, you are feeling relaxed and positive. Feeling just fine.

**43**

# Maslow's Hierarchy of Needs

**As a paramedic, police officer, firefighter, or rescue worker, you will initially be managing victims who are in a <u>survival mode</u>.**

Psychologist Abraham Maslow developed a model to illustrate that most people move up a hierarchy of needs as lower needs are satisfied.

For example, people recently devastated by a hurricane are primarily concerned with their immediate physical sur-vival needs for water, food, shelter, and sleep.

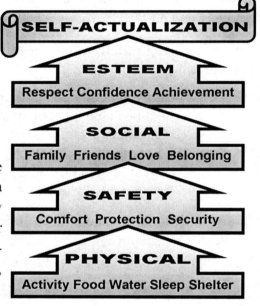

**SELF-ACTUALIZATION**

**ESTEEM**
Respect Confidence Achievement

**SOCIAL**
Family Friends Love Belonging

**SAFETY**
Comfort Protection Security

**PHYSICAL**
Activity Food Water Sleep Shelter

Once these basic needs are satisfied, they can begin to think longer term. They then start to consider safety, comfort, and health. Next is their connection or relationship needs. The higher the level, the longer they see into their future.

---

**Maslow also created this Four Stages of Learning Model:**

- ► Unconscious Incompetence (not knowing that you cannot ride a bike)
- ► Conscious Incompetence (knowing that you cannot ride a bike)
- ► Conscious Competence (knowing that you know how to ride the bike)
- ► Unconscious Competence (totally oblivious about how well you ride that bike)

## What this model means for emergency responders

**The first order of business for a first responder is to ensure that the scene is safe before attending to an injured person.**

Be aware that patients' priorities may be significantly different than yours. Once your patients' first level **Physical** needs are met, they can move on to **Safety** needs. As their condition improves and stabilizes, they will likely move on to higher level needs.

Because lower needs are associated with survival, there is a good chance that people at this stage will be in a light trance. This means there is Critical Faculty Bypass, and therefore are highly suggestible. Their senses are highly acute, and they're desperately looking for someone to help them.

Your uniform identifies you as someone in a position to help. Your words carry a lot of weight. Uniformed or not, how you interact with your patient can make the difference in just getting by or getting the reassurance they anxiously need.

---

### Like all models, this one is imperfect.
#### *Please approach it with a sense of flexibility.*

For instance, some people are very happy living on the street – that's where their friends are. Some people may rate their life's obsession more important than food.

Think of the starving musician or artist. Monks have been known to sacrifice their comfort needs in order to reach self-actualization.

---

45

# Communication Styles

**Confusion and misunderstandings happen for many reasons.**

People communicate in various styles, almost as if they are speaking different languages. Knowing how these different styles clash can help put your ideas across more clearly and give your opinion greater acceptance.

Like the other models I am sharing with you, I will explain this one with sufficient depth for you to understand the essential concepts. In practical terms, just reading the next few pages will not give you enough information to employ this model at your next emergency.

As with most abilities, your communication skills will quickly improve with practice. To begin, apply these concepts in your everyday communication at work and at home. In time, your improved capability and skill will carry over to your work in the field during traumatic and stressful situations.

There are many communication models. This particular model, from the field of Neurolinguistic Programming (NLP), is commonly known as VAK (*Visual, Auditory, and Kinesthetic*).

The full VAK model is quite detailed, so I will just provide a brief overview here. As we begin to explore VAK, remember that, as with other models, all of us possess varying mixtures of all styles.

> **NLP could be the most important synthesis of knowledge about human communication... to emerge since the explosion of humanistic psychology in the sixties.**
> *Science Digest*

To better understand this communications model, study the characteristics of the three styles shown on the next few pages. Then take the self-audit on pages 63 through 73. In the following days, observe your family, friends, and colleagues. Soon you will notice the patterns in their communication styles.

To enhance your communication with others, match their particular style. For example, if you know that the other person is kinesthetic, and you are visual, slow down your speech and use the words that kinesthetic communicators use.

Instead of:  *I see what you're looking for.*

Use:  *Now I've got a handle about what you want to uncover.*

You can find out more about this communications model on YouTube and other online resources.

My own YouTube video is at www.ERcommSkills.com

## Try This at Home

*Want to communicate better with your spouse and children?*
  Determine if they are V, A, or K. Then communicate in words that they respond to and use.

# Visual Communicators

## CHARACTERISTICS

- breathe high in the chest
- may have difficulty with verbal instructions
- gesture up with their hand
- have a higher-pitched voice
- are neat and orderly
- lift up their head
- look up when talking
- are organized and observant
- prefer to read rather than be read to
- not usually distracted by noise
- stand erect - shoulders straight across
- stand back - so as to "take it all in"
- remember what they see, rather than hear
- must see to learn

## WORDS THEY USE AND RESPOND TO

- I **see** what you mean
- **Looking** ahead
- You'll **look** back at this and laugh
- The future looks **bright**
- It **appears** to me
- This will shed some **light** on the matter
- Taking a dim **view**
- **Sight** for sore eyes
- Mind's **eye**
- It colors his **view** of life
- I am **looking** closely at the idea
- I have a **hazy** notion
- Beyond a **shadow** of a doubt

48

# Auditory Communicators

## CHARACTERISTICS

- ◆ are great orators - speak clearly
- ◆ are easily distracted by noise
- ◆ are talkative - love their own voice
- ◆ tilt their head as if on the phone
- ◆ hold their shoulders back
- ◆ have rhythmic breathing  - sigh -
- ◆ learn by listening
- ◆ drum their fingers or tap their toes
- ◆ move eyes from side-to-side or down left
- ◆ have difficulty with written directions
- ◆ talk to themselves while thinking
- ◆ remember conversations well

## WORDS THEY USE AND RESPOND TO

- ◆ **Loud** & clear
- ◆ It **rings a bell**
- ◆ In a manner of **speaking**
- ◆ Un**heard**-of
- ◆ Turn a **deaf** ear
- ◆ That's all **Greek** to me
- ◆ On the same **wavelength**
- ◆ **Music** to my **ears**
- ◆ Living in **harmony**
- ◆ He's **calling** the **tune**
- ◆ **Tell**-me
- ◆ A lot of **mumbo-jumbo**
- ◆ **Sounds** good
- ◆ **rings**-true

49

# Kinesthetic Communicators

## CHARACTERISTICS

- well coordinated - have athletic abilities
- breathe low and deep in the abdomen
- have a low pitch voice and slower tone
- speak slowly and use action words
- can't sit still for long periods (antsy)
- stand close when talking
- have gut feelings
- gesture down by their middle or stomach
- point to their heart
- look down to their right
- want to act things out
- touch people to get their attention
- may have messy handwriting

## WORDS THEY USE AND RESPOND TO

- Got a **handle** on
- Get a **hold** of yourself
- **Hang** in there
- **Thick**-skinned
- Out of **touch**
- Make **contact**
- **Hand** in **hand**
- I can **grasp** that idea
- **Show** me what you mean
- **Hold** on a second
- I will get in **touch** with you
- **Scratch** the surface
- I can't **put** my finger on it

# Communication Styles
## are also
## *Learning Styles*

If you have difficulty absorbing new material, perhaps you are not using your primary communication channel. You will learn more about your own style once you complete the self-audit beginning on page 63.

Understanding this concept and employing it on the job might influence your career advancement. Match your style with the learning tips given in the diagram below.

**VISUAL**

Color-coding your notes
Use pictures and diagrams
Use charts for outlines and note taking
Remember what you <u>see</u>, rather than hear
Spelling is improved by visualizing words
Memorize using pictures / concept maps

**AUDITORY**

Record information & play back
Participate in discussions
Have someone read to you
Practice by asking questions
Listen to Baroque music
Read aloud

**KINESTHETIC**

Focus on experiential activities:
role-playing & lab work
Take many breaks while studying
Remember by tracing letters & words
Memorize better through...
walking, dancing, exercising
Learn by experiencing and doing
Act things out - role play

# The Stages of Grieving

**Why mention grieving here?**

When someone close to us dies, a relationship breaks up, or we get fired, we usually go through several stages of grieving. This "Stages of Grieving" concept was first developed in 1969 by psychiatrist Dr. Elisabeth Kübler-Ross.

**The same stages of grieving can occur when someone faces a traumatic situation.** When interacting with injured persons or their distressed families, knowledge of this grieving process can be most helpful.

A curious question or an irrational statement may simply be an expression of one of these stages. Although you will have to respond on the spot in your own manner, **your knowledge of these stages will prepare you for how a victim may act or react**.

As a seasoned professional with extensive expertise in crisis situations, please be aware that you too might experience some forms of grieving during or after tending to a victim.

These steps may be experienced in any order, some may be repeated, and some will be transitory.

| | |
|---|---|
| **Denial** | This can't be happening to me. |
| **Anger** | Why me? <br> Damn that other driver. |
| **Bargaining** | Please God, let me live <br> (take away the hurt) and I'll... |
| **Depression** | I wish I were dead. <br> *Victim feels a lack of control, hopelessness, and numbness.* |
| **Acceptance** | OK, it happened – *Now on with my life.* |

# Language Patterns and Embedded Commands

When people are anxious or angry, they may have a tendency to reject some or all of a direct instruction. Sometimes, telling an angry person to calm down or telling someone who is anxious to cheer up just does not work.

**If you sense some resistance**, the direct pattern may result in non-compliance. Indirect patterns, by their very nature, are stealth. Since a trauma victim is likely in a light trance and may have Critical Faculty Bypass, indirect patterns can be extremely effective.

Just before we move on to some creative ways to incorporate Indirect Language, here is one brilliant example found in my neighborhood coffee shop:

> **Unattended children will receive free Espresso!**

### Remember the story of the car salesman?

He used a tricky phrase:

There has never been a better time to…
*buy a car on Saturday.*

This is an NLP pattern known as an *embedded command*.
Read on...

**53**

## Embedded Commands

This technique can be combined with Indirect Language patterns. Embedded means that, within an apparently innocent sentence, you are able to <u>hide a direct command</u>. Even if the Conscious Mind fails to pick up the suggestion, the Subconscious Mind will certainly heed the instruction.

The technique, known as *Analog Marking*, is used to deliberately cause a break in your sentence with a short pause, before you deliver the embedded command in a lower tone and slightly increased or decreased volume, tempo, or intensity.

The pause creates a minor ambiguity in meaning and causes the Subconscious Mind to pay attention.

The key here is to repeat the <u>command part</u> a few times. For instance, if an agitated person needs to relax, and is not responding to your Direct Language, use a few of the examples found on the next page. The Indirect patterns are the Set Up phrases, with the embedded commands in the right column.

**To master this concept**, study these patterns. Then, look for opportunities to test them out on your children and their friends. It may seen artificial at first, but with a bit of practice you will notice your wishes being granted more often.

With this practice in your personal life, these patterns may suddenly show up when you're tending to your patient.

| The Set Up | | Embedded Command |
|---|---|---|
| *Say this first* | | *Say with changed speed, tempo, and tone* |
| Think about a time when you were lying on the beach with the sun on your face.<br>Remember how... | **P**<br><br>**A** | YOU<br><br>ARE<br><br>SO<br><br>RELAXED |
| Once we get you to the hospital, you will know that... | | |
| Remember after a hard day's work, you get home, sit in your favorite chair, and put up your feet.  Think of that now, and see how ... | | |
| As you take a deep breath, just feel how your body slowly and gradually can... | **U** | LET GO OF<br>THE TENSIONS |
| I don't know when... | **S** | YOU WILL<br>FEEL BETTER |
| Perhaps you'll... | **E** | FEEL BETTER NOW |
| As you begin to breathe more slowly, you may begin to notice how... | | YOUR SHOULDERS<br>ARE MORE RELAXED |
| You look/sound like... | | YOU ARE FEELING BETTER |
| Take this. It will make you... | | FEEL MORE<br>COMFORTABLE |

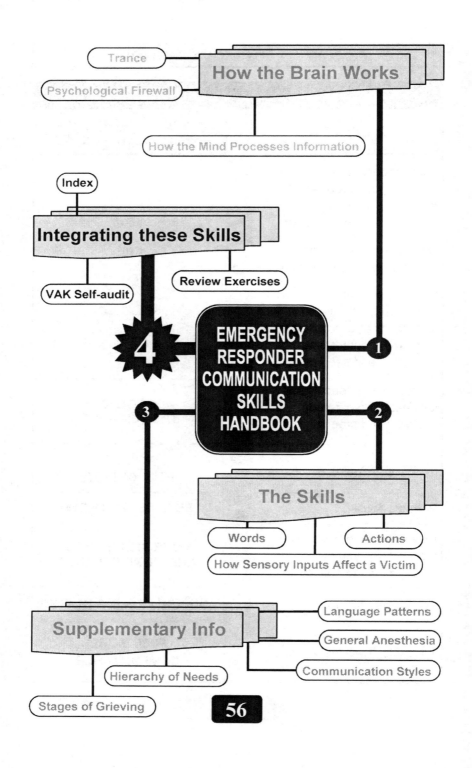

Trance

Psychological Firewall

**How the Brain Works**

How the Mind Processes Information

Index

**Integrating these Skills**

VAK Self-audit

Review Exercises

4

EMERGENCY
RESPONDER
COMMUNICATION
SKILLS
HANDBOOK

1

3

2

**The Skills**

Words

Actions

How Sensory Inputs Affect a Victim

Language Patterns

General Anesthesia

Communication Styles

**Supplementary Info**

Hierarchy of Needs

Stages of Grieving

# Integrating these Skills

# REVIEW EXERCISES

*In order to help you integrate the information found in this handbook, I have provided two exercises. The answers are on page 62.*

*In addition on pages 63 through 73, you will find a Communication Style Self-Audit .*

Visit our website for additional resources
### www.ERcommSkills.com

---

1. The mind is a _____ that regulates the flow of energy and information.

2. Awareness of your thoughts and experiences is a description of your _____ Mind.

3. Patterns (habits) are located in the _____ Mind.

4. The period of personality development before the age of seven is known as the _____ Phase.

5. Self-preservation is of paramount importance to the _____ Mind.

6. The psychological firewall is known as the _____ _____.

7. In effect, a child's perception is:
   Your ideas = My _____.

---

8. To help a client enter a trance a hypnotherapist uses a combination of _____attention, _____ , relaxation, and/or _____.

9. A person can drift into trance through repetitive beats. Give some examples

_____

_____

_____

10. When people are in trance, anything they hear goes directly into their Subconscious Mind as a _____ to be followed.

11. A patient in an agitated emotional state is in fact in a light trance, and therefore _____-_____.

12. Distressed persons are in a light trance and therefore their Critical Faculty has been _____.

13. Non-verbal cues include voice _____, gestures, _____ expressions, and _____.

14. Everything patients hear, see, smell, taste, and feel can be _____ by their active imagination.

15. This is called Awfulizing or _____.

16. Most mental processing is _____.

17. The Subconscious Mind interprets and responds to information _____.

18. When someone is in a trance, their senses are highly _____.

19. Stress is often a result of people's perception of their lack of _____.

20. When using embedded commands, the pause creates a minor _____ in meaning, and causes the Subconscious Mind to _____.

21. The stages of grieving are

        D_____

        A_____

        B_____

        D_____

        A_____

22. Most of the time, our breathing is quite _____.

## Visual, Auditory, or Kinesthetic Characteristics?

| 1 | are talkative - love their own voice | |
|---|---|---|
| 2 | have gut feelings | |
| 3 | have rhythmic breathing  - sigh - | |
| 4 | may have difficulty with verbal instructions | |
| 5 | learn by listening | |
| 6 | may have difficulty with written directions | |
| 7 | stand back - so as to "take it all in" | |
| 8 | remember conversations well | |
| 9 | can't sit still for long periods (antsy) | |
| 10 | drum their fingers or tap their toes | |
| 11 | touch people to get their attention | |
| 12 | are well coordinated and have athletic abilities | |
| 13 | talk to themselves while thinking | |
| 14 | are easily distracted by noise | |
| 15 | stand close when talking | |
| 16 | point to, or put hand on, their heart | |
| 17 | have a low pitch voice and slower tone | |
| 18 | breathe high in the chest | |
| 19 | point to their ear | |
| 20 | have a higher-pitched voice, speak quickly | |
| 21 | tilt their head as if on the phone | |
| 22 | breathe low and deep in the abdomen | |
| 23 | are good mechanically | |
| 24 | speak slowly and use action words | |

## Answers to the fill-in-the-blanks exercise

1. process
2. Conscious
3. Subconscious
4. Imprint
5. Subconscious
6. Critical Faculty
7. reality
8. focused   progressive   confusion
9. drumming, flashing lights, chanting, music
10. suggestion or direction
11. hyper-suggestible or highly suggestible
12. bypassed
13. cadence & tone   facial   posture
14. exaggerated or amplified
15. Catastrophizing
16. visual
17. literally
18. acute
19. control
20. ambiguity   pay attention
21. Denial, Anger, Bargaining, Depression, Acceptance
22. shallow

## Answers to the VAK exercise

| | | | | | | | |
|---|---|---|---|---|---|---|---|
| 1 | A | 7 | V | 13 | A | 19 | A |
| 2 | K | 8 | A | 14 | A | 20 | V |
| 3 | A | 9 | K | 15 | K | 21 | A |
| 4 | V or K | 10 | A or K | 16 | K | 22 | K |
| 5 | A | 11 | K | 17 | K | 23 | K |
| 6 | A or K | 12 | K | 18 | V | 24 | K |

# VAK

## Visual Auditory Kinesthetic
## Communication Style
## Self-Audit

The following personal survey is designed to
discover your primary communication channel.

Your channel simply sheds light
on how you relate as a human being,
*and it reveals how you run your relationships.*

♦♦♦♦♦♦♦♦

Since you may interact with others differently
at home, work, and socially, first complete this
survey in only <u>one of those three contexts.</u>
Complete it in the other contexts at separate times.

♦♦♦♦♦♦♦♦

Answer each question with
the first response that comes to mind.

If an answer does not immediately come to mind, do it later.
Do only as many as required to notice your pattern.

♦♦♦♦♦♦♦♦

Keep track on a separate piece of paper
with three columns headed V A K.

**When I love someone, I get an instant experience of**
- V. The way we look together - the eyes of love
- A. The sound of telling him or her or being told, I love you
- K. A feeling or sense of warmth toward that person

**My first memory is of:**
- V. Looking at something
- A. Being spoken to
- K. Doing something

**If I am angry, I tend to:**
- V. Keep replaying in my mind what it is that has upset me
- A. Raise my voice and tell people how I feel
- K. Stamp about, slam doors and physically demonstrate my anger

**I get along better with people who:**
- V. Relate to the world through the way it looks
- A. Relate to the world through the way it sounds
- K. Relate to the world through the way it makes them feel

**When I experience anxiety, the very first thing that happens is:**
- V. The world takes on a different appearance in some way
- A. Sounds begin to bother me
- K. My sense of ease begins to alter

**When I get totally motivated, the first thing that happens is:**
- V. I see things from a new resourceful perspective
- A. I tell myself how this state is going to create new possibilities
- K. I can actually feel myself getting psyched up

At the gym, my satisfaction comes first from:
- V. Seeing myself in the mirror getting better
- A. Hearing myself or others say how good I'm looking
- K. Feeling my body get stronger and sensing it's more in shape

When I engage in my favorite sport,
I particularly enjoy:
- V. The look of the game, or how I look playing it
- A. The sound of the game, such as the thwack of the ball, or the roar of the crowd
- K. The feel of the game, such as the grip of the club or the sense of motion

The subject I enjoyed the most in school
came about primarily as a result of:
- V. The way it looked on the board or in books
- A. The sound of the subject as it was taught to me
- K. My sense of interest as I learned more about it

During my free time I most enjoy:
- V. Going to museums and galleries
- A. Listening to music and talking to my friends
- K. Playing sport

Death, for me, is probably:
- V. To see no more, or to see in a totally new way
- A. To hear no more, or to hear in a totally new way
- K. To feel no more, or to feel in a totally new way

Having rapport with someone is:
- V. Seeing him or her in a wonderful and easy-to-be-with way
- A. Hearing the person communicate things exactly the way I would
- K. Feeling toward the person the way I know he or she feels toward me

Having a conversation at a party,
my whole frame of experience will change if:
- V. The lights get brighter or dimmer
- A. The music changes pace
- K. The room temperature changes

When I have occasion to use mathematics,
I verify my answer by:
- V. Looking at the numbers to see if they look correct
- A. Counting the numbers in my head
- K. Using my fingers to get a sense of correctness

If I am choosing food off a menu, I tend to:
- V. Imagine what the food will look like
- A. Talk through the options in my head or with my partner
- K. Imagine what the food will taste like

When I operate new equipment I generally:
- V. Read the instructions first
- A. Listen to an explanation from someone who has used it before
- K. Go ahead and have a go, I can figure it out as I use it

When you recall a time you were immensely drawn to someone, what was the very best thing that attracted you to this person? Was It:
- V. The way this person looked
- A. Something he/she said to you, or that you heard
- K. The way he/she touched you, something you felt

When I am choosing a holiday I usually:
- V. Read lots of brochures
- A. Listen to recommendations from friends
- K. Imagine what it would be like to be there

**Most of my free time is spent:**
- V. Watching television
- A. Talking to friends
- K. Doing physical activity or making things

**When I get an assignment at work,**
**it is easier to understand and to execute if:**
- V. It's written or diagrammed
- A. It's explained to me
- K. I get a sense of clarity, purpose, or correctness from it

**If I have to complain about faulty goods,**
**I am most comfortable:**
- V. Writing a letter
- A. Complaining over the phone
- K. Taking the item back to the store or posting it to head office

**I choose household furnishings because I like:**
- V. Their colors and how they look
- A. The descriptions the sales-people give me
- K. Their textures & what it feels like to touch them

**I really love:**
- V. Watching films, photography, looking at art or people watching
- A. Listening to music, or talking to friends
- K. Taking part in sporting activities, eating fine foods and wines or dancing

**When I turn off to someone,**
**I get an immediate experience of dislike.**
- V. When I see him or her approach
- A. When he or she begins talking to me
- K. When I sense him or her nearby

**Before going to sleep at night, it's important that:**
- V. The room is nearly dark or pleasantly shaded
- A. The room is hushed or muted with pleasing background quiet
- K. The bed feels very comfortable

**When I first contact a new person, I usually:**
- V. Arrange a face to face meeting
- A. Talk to him or her on the telephone
- K. Suggest we meet at an activity or meal

**In the morning, I especially enjoy awakening to:**
- V. Either the sun streaming in or an overcast day
- A. The sound of a lively wind or rain pelting the windows
- K. A warm and toasty comforter or flannel sheets

**When I listen to a band, I can't help:**
- V. Watching the band members and other people in the audience
- A. Listening to the lyrics and the beats
- K. Moving in time with the music

**When I have to prepare for a meeting or exam, I generally:**
- V. Write lots of revision notes and diagrams
- A. Talk over my notes, alone or with other people
- K. Imagine making the movement or creating the formula

**I find It easier to be with my friends if:**
- V. They communicate using animation and to-the-point statements
- A. They interact with me through easy-to-hear and varying speech
- K. I get a feeling that they know where I'm coming from

**When you drive, how do you navigate?**
- V. I look for road signs or follow a map of the territory
- A. I listen for familiar sounds that point me in the right direction
- K. I get a gut feeling or sense of where I am

**When I need directions for traveling I usually:**
- V. Look at a map
- A. Ask for spoken directions
- K. Follow my nose and maybe use a compass

**I know my career is taking a turn for the better when:**
- V. I see myself moving into the corner office
- A. I hear the boss say, "You're going to go places"
- K. I feel satisfaction in getting a promotion

**When I concentrate, I most often:**
- V. Focus on the words or the pictures in front of me
- A. Discuss the problem and the possible solutions in my head
- K. Move around a lot, fiddle with pens and pencils and touch things

**I remember things best by:**
- V. Writing notes or keeping printed details
- A. Saying them aloud or repeating words and key points in my head
- K. Doing and practicing the activity or imagining it being done

**When my problems get me down, I find it helps to:**
- V. Write them down so I can see them clearly
- A. Talk or listen to another until my problems sound easier to hear
- K. Sort them out internally until they make sense

On the occasions when I think of a former lover, the very first thing I do is:
- V. See the person in my mind's eye
- A. Hear his or her voice in my mind
- K. Get a certain feeling about the person

When I meet an old friend:
- V. I say "it's great to see you!"
- A. I say "it's great to hear from you!"
- K. I give them a hug or a handshake

I first notice how people:
- V. Look and dress
- A. Sound and speak
- K. Stand and move

I tend to say:
- V. I see what you mean
- A. I hear what you are saying
- K. I know how you feel

I think that you can tell if someone is lying if:
- V. He or she avoids looking at you
- A. His or her voice changes
- K. He or she gives you funny vibes

When someone tells me, "I love you", my first experience is:
- V. An image of the person loving me, or us together
- A. A dialogue within my soul saying, "This is wonderful"
- K. A feeling of pleasurable contentment

If I was buying a new car, I would:
- V. Read reviews in newspapers and magazines
- A. Discuss what I need with my friends
- K. Test-drive lots of different types

When I am anxious, I:
  V. Visualize the worst-case scenarios
  A. Talk over in my head what worries me most
  K. Can't sit still, fiddle and move around constantly

Which group do I tend to favor:
  V. Photography, painting, reading, sketching, films
  A. Music, musical instruments, the sound of the sea, wind chimes, concerts
  K. Ball games, woodworking, massage, introspection, touching

When I spell, I verify accuracy by:
  V. Looking at the word in my mind's eye to see if it looks the way that word should
  A. Saying the word out loud or hearing it in my mind
  K. Getting a feeling about how the word is spelled

When I make decisions, it helps to:
  V. Picture the possible choices in my mind's eye
  A. Hear both sides of a dialogue within my mind
  K. Sense how I would feel if either choice came to pass

If I am explaining to someone I tend to:
  V. Show him or her what I mean
  A. Explain to him or her in different ways until he or she understands
  K. Encourage him or her to talk through my idea as he or she applies it

I remember things best by:
  V. Writing notes or keeping printed details
  A. Saying them aloud or repeating words and key points in my head
  K. Doing and practicing the activity or imagining it being done

**When I go shopping for clothes, I tend to:**
- V. Imagine what they would look like on
- A. Discuss them with the shop staff
- K. Put them on and test them out

**I find it easiest to remember:**
- V. Faces
- A. Names
- K. Things I have done

**When I am learning a new skill, I am most comfortable:**
- V. Watching what the teacher is doing
- A. Talking through with the teacher exactly what I'm supposed to do
- K. Giving it a try myself and work it out as I go

**When I'm very happy, my world:**
- V. Takes on a definite and wonderful shine
- A. Resonates with total harmony
- K. Fits perfectly within the space of my life

**When I cook a new dish, I like to:**
- V. Follow a written recipe
- A. Call a friend for an explanation
- K. Follow my instincts, testing as I cook

**When you recall a particularly wonderful vacation you had, what's the very first experience you remember?**
- V. The way the resort area looked
- A. The different way it sounded to you
- K. The feeling you got by vacationing there

At the beach, the very first thing that makes me glad to be there is:
V. The look of the sand, the smiling sun, and the ice-blue water
A. The sound of the waves, the laughing wind, and distant whispers
K. The feel of the sand, the salt air on my lips, and the joy of serenity

If I am teaching someone something new, I tend to:
V. Write instructions down for this person
A. Give this person a verbal explanation
K. Demonstrate first, and then let him or her have a turn

I feel especially connected to other people because:
V. How they look
A. What they say to me
K. How they make me feel

During sex, I like to:
V. Look at what's going on
A. Hear my lover
K. Feel every sensation

When I spell, I verify accuracy by:
V. Looking at the word in my mind's eye to see if it looks the way that word should
A. Saying the word out loud or hearing it in my mind
K. Getting a feeling about how it's spelled

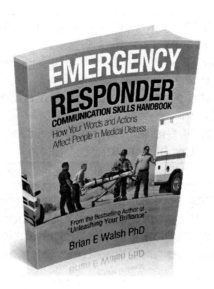

For bulk purchase of this Handbook, contact

Office@ERcommSkills.com

**1 866 385 3848**
Toll-free in Canada & USA

---

If you would like to provide input for
the next revision of this Handbook,
contact the publisher directly:

Office@ERcommSkills.com

---

# What They're Saying

**Emergency Responder Communication Skills Handbook** is a much needed resource. Since the physical needs of casualties are so urgent and dire, it is easy to overlook the severity of their mental and emotional needs. Dr. Walsh's work here brings that to the responders' attention and gives them extremely valuable tools for treating the entire person, helping to alleviate some of their traumatic response, and giving them the tools to heal.

Having served for years in law enforcement and subsequently teaching at the academy, I have a unique perspective of officers dealing with emergencies. I believe that the content of Dr. Walsh's communication skills handbook is a valuable asset that every officer should own.

*Dr. Darlene Silvernail PhD CAP DAC LMHC*

---

I found the information in Dr. Walsh's **Emergency Responder Communication Skills Handbook** to be enlightening and very relevant to the job of a paramedic, or any first responder for that matter.

It brought to mind a call that I had done years ago when I first started in the EMS field. We had just brought an unconscious trauma patient into the emergency department at the local Trauma Centre. I made a comment to the Emergency Room Physician about the severity of the patient's condition. The Physician took me out into the hall and explained that I should be careful with what I say in front of unconscious patients. He went on to tell me about a patient they once had in ICU who had been unconscious for a period of time. Once the patient regained consciousness, he thanked all those who had encouraged him and wished him well while he was unconscious because, although he couldn't respond, he could hear them. I never forgot that bit of information, and Dr. Walsh's book only reinforces that point for me.

*Jim Christie, Operations Manager, PCP, A-EMCA*

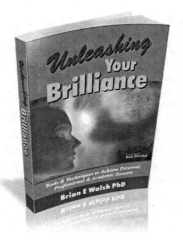

# Guided Self-Hypnosis Audio CDs

# Index

| | |
|---|---|
| Abdominal breathing | 50 |
| Accelerated learning | vi vii viii |
| Acceptance | 52 |
| Analytical | 6 9 |
| Anger | 25 52 |
| Auditory | 35 46 51 |
| Awfulizing | 34 37 |
| Bargaining | 52 |
| Blanket | 21 |
| Body language | 22 23 |
| Bystanders | 26 38 39 |
| Catastrophizing | 34 37 |
| Characteristics of our Minds | 5 9 |
| Conscious Mind | 4 - 9 |
| Critical Faculty | 10 - 15 19 20 37 45 53 |
| Defensive filters | 4 |

| | |
|---|---|
| Denial | 52 |
| Depression | 52 |
| Direct language | 30 31 |
| Embedded Commands | 53 55 |
| Emotions | 8 10 13 |
| Facial expressions | 21 - 23 |
| General Anesthesia | 38 39 |
| Grieving | 52 |
| Habits | 8 |
| Humor | vii 33 |
| Hypnotherapy | 3 6 13 42 |
| Hypnotic induction | 13 |
| Imprint Phase | 8 10 12 |
| Indirect Language | 30 31 53 - 55 |
| Kinesthetic | 42 46 47 50 51 |
| Kübler-Ross | 52 |

| | |
|---|---|
| Learning Styles | 51 |
| Linear & Logical | 6 |
| Maslow's Hierarchy of Needs | 44  45 |
| Mind Maps | viii  ix |
| Name (using person's) | 26 |
| Negative words | 28  29 |
| Neurolinguistic Programming (NLP) | 46 - 51 |
| Subconscious Mind | 3 - 5<br>7 - 10<br>13 - 15<br>19  20<br>22  28<br>35 - 38<br>42  43 |
| Non-verbal cues | 22  23 |
| Paraphrase | 27 |
| Patterns (habits) | 3  8  9<br>13  26 |
| Patterns (language) | 30  31<br>47<br>53 - 55 |
| Permanent memory | viii 7<br>8  12 |

| | |
|---|---|
| Position changes | 38  39 |
| Psychological Firewall<br>... see Critical Faculty | |
| Rationality | 7  9 |
| Review Exercises | 58 - 61 |
| Sensory Inputs | 36 - 39 |
| Stress | 20 - 22<br>35  38<br>46  52 |
| Technical jargon | 26  35 |
| Temporary Memory | 6  9 |
| Touch | 4  21<br>23 |
| Trance | 3<br>13  14<br>19  35<br>37  45<br>53 |
| Uniform | 19  45 |
| V A K | 46 - 51 |
| VAK Self-audit | 61 - 71 |
| Visual | 46 - 48<br>51 |
| Willpower | 6  9 |